DECOUPAGE

BY **LESLIE LINSLEY**

PHOTOGRAPHY BY JON ARON

DECOUPAGE

A NEW LOOK AT AN OLD CRAFT

DOUBLEDAY & COMPANY, INC., GARDEN CITY, NEW YORK

LIBRARY OF CONGRESS CARD CATALOG NUMBER 73–168290

COPYRIGHT © 1972 BY LESLIE LINSLEY

ALL RIGHTS RESERVED

PRINTED IN THE UNITED STATES OF AMERICA

9   8   7   6   5   4   3

CONTENTS

*Half-round treasure box
handmade by Gramp, designed
by Leslie Linsley.*

INTRODUCTION TO DECOUPAGE

A few years ago when I told people I was a craftsman in the art of decoupage, they would say: "Decotage? What's that?" or "Declotage? It sounds immoral," or "Deglopage? Is that a new hippy art form?" However, just three years later decoupage has become so popular that it rarely needs an explanation.

Decoupage is an eighteenth-century craft. From the French, it means, "applied cutouts." Decoupage was inspired by the lacquer furniture imported from China and Japan. Fine furniture was elaborately decorated with cutouts from prints that were hand-colored. An artist who does decoupage is called a decoupeur, but I despise that word so much that I prefer to be called a craftsman in the art of decoupage.

Today, the cutout designs are usually applied to wood, in the form of furniture, plaques, trays or boxes. Decoupage can also be done on metal or glass, but my most successful experiences have been with wooden objects.

It is not necessary to have any formal training to do this craft. For that matter, one need not be terribly talented to learn the technique. The process of decoupage can be learned by reading a few simple "how to" instructions. Once you have learned the technique of decoupage you can apply your own creativity.

For several years I have been working on wooden boxes and decorating them with decoupage without having had any formal training from either book or class. My mother learned it from a friend, and I learned the process from her. After having done it for some time I decided to do a little research on the subject. Much to my horror, I discovered that everything written about this eighteenth-century art was so complicated and involved that had I first read about it before doing it, my career as a decoupage artist would never have come about. I therefore decided that someday I would write a simple how-to book on decoupage. That was about a year ago, and now decoupage is so popular it seems the time is right. There is an even more important reason for writing this book: creativity. It is in this area that I believe decoupage has its greatest potential.

There has been so much emphasis placed on technique that there has been little creativity related to decoupage. There is so much room to be creative that I hope you'll think about this aspect before you begin your first piece. This doesn't mean that you have to be an artist. When you were a child you had a certain amount of spontaneity in expressing yourself. Perhaps something that appealed to you as a child is a good beginning. Something from the past that you particularly liked—a tree that you picnicked under, the first flower a boy ever gave you. Create a scene in your head. It may spark off an idea for a design. I don't, for instance, think that pasting an entire picture on a box is creative decoupage even though it is a good way to learn the techniques of pasting and finishing.

In this age of instant everything, there is also instant decoupage. There are many spray varnishes and lacquers on the market. There are also decals that are precut. It seems to me that with the traditional craft of decoupage, it is a shame to take the craftsmanship out of it and give it a plastic look. (On the other hand, it is just as wrong, in my opinion, to make decoupage more complicated than it is.) So, as we go on together learning decoupage, think creatively. Force yourself to take time to look at things. Everything can bring about ideas.

I was just finishing this book when I was invited to teach decoupage aboard the *Queen Elizabeth 2*. I couldn't think of a nicer way to teach and work on a manuscript than cruising in the Caribbean. Besides, I could get all kinds of ideas from the ladies who joined the group. The most outstanding thing I learned was that if sixty women are given the same printed cutouts and the same little wooden boxes, at the end of two weeks you will have sixty finished boxes each of which is completely different. Each person looked at her materials and arranged them in a way that was appealing to her. It was terrific. I think I learned more from them than they did from me. And so . . . as I sit here in my studio varnishing, with antiquing all over my elbow, I am making a note of every possible helpful hint that pops into my head so that anybody can successfully learn to decoupage.

Designs for this box were cut from an old children's nursery book.

Handmade card box decoupaged with delicate blackberries.

SUMMARY OF PROCESS

A short summary of the process of decoupage seems important so that you will know briefly what you're in for before getting swamped with detail.

The process involved is this:

1. Sand and paint the item you have chosen to decoupage. It might be a plaque of wood or a box or tray or even a piece of furniture.

2. After painting, you will lightly sand and repeat this painting and sanding process four or five times. If the item is tiny, like this trinket box, four times should be enough.

3. Next, you will cut a design from paper or choose a picture that is the right size to be pasted on your object to form a pleasing design. This could be a scene from a book.

4. Then you will apply several coats of varnish over the paper design that has been glued to your object. Each coat of varnish will dry overnight before sanding lightly between coats. You will apply approximately ten coats or more of varnish, depending on how thick or thin your paper is. The varnish will cover your design with a clear hard finish so that it becomes part of the surface of the piece you are working on.

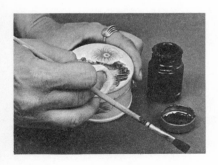

5. You can then antique the object, but this is optional.

6. The whole piece is then rubbed with steel wool, waxed and buffed.

Now that we've established the process, let's get started.

WHAT TO DECOUPAGE

The first decision to make is what to decoupage. I have found that decoupage is best applied to wood. The most frequently used article to decoupage is a wooden plaque—a good item to do as a first project. There is only one surface to work on, it is flat and you can use a fairly large picture, which might be easier to find and cut out than anything else.

I have seen decoupage done on a dresser top, coffee table, even a wooden counter top, which a friend of mine did as a first project. Such an area is a big undertaking for the first attempt, but the result was effective, reflecting individual interests. An excellent cook, she had used recipes and different food pictures from *Gourmet* magazine.

If you decide to put pictures on a wooden plaque, the boards could be cut and beveled on the edges at a lumberyard. If you wanted to make a grouping for the kitchen, you could apply fruit or flower pictures to individual boards (however many you wanted) and the finished boards could be hung by brass rings that screw into the top of each board. These rings can be purchased for under fifty cents apiece in a frame shop, hardware or art supply store. It would be smart to figure out what your subject matter will be and how big a board you will need for your picture, as you would a picture frame, and take the exact measurements to the lumberyard. If you want to be sure that the size you choose will be right for your wall space, you could cut out a pattern of the exact size from plain paper and tape it in place on the wall.

My mother did a plaque for her kitchen. She found an oval board that had been used for something else. It was in good shape and already beveled around the edge. She thought perhaps it could double as a cheeseboard and decoration. With cutouts she created a barnyard scene. The background is white and the border, yellow. I don't think you could cut cheese on it, but it could be used for serving. In any event, it makes a delightful kitchen ornament.

You might want to decoupage the knobs on a dresser for a start and eventually a piece of furniture. Picture frames

Wooden switch plate by Ruth Linsley.

Cheeseboard with barnyard scene by Ruth Linsley.

are interesting, perhaps a small desk top, a mirror or an old trunk. You might consider a light-switch plate, which you could decorate by cutting out a design from the wallpaper in the room. For holidays, wooden napkin rings could be made for your own table or as a gift. I think holly berries would be a lovely design for a Christmas table. My favorite is a box, and boxes are not too difficult to find. I think boxes are the most appealing because they can be made to use for anything, anywhere, and besides I am fortunate to have a grandfather who makes all of my boxes by hand. But we all can't be that lucky. I strongly advise against cigar boxes because they are not good enough to be used for such beautiful work. In the event that the piece should turn out spectacularly great, it would be a shame to have put all that work into a cigar box that will eventually fall apart.

Old-fashioned towel rack can have a border of decoupage.

14

*Inexpensive wooden napkin rings
are a good, small project.*

Where to Find Boxes

You could make a box yourself. (See *Where to Find Things*.) The box could be made of pine, birchwood or plywood. Almost any wood would do because you will coat the box with so many layers of paint and varnish that you will have covered up any imperfections in the wood. A box that you make yourself could be very charming even, perhaps especially, if it isn't perfect. However, if you aren't handy at carpentry, you could find boxes in the following places.

Keep an eye out in antique shops, thrift shops, Goodwill and garage sales for wooden boxes that aren't too big. If your first project is too large, it will become discouraging. Often I have found old recipe file boxes for the kitchen or my desk that are fun to do.

You might also want to consider working on a new box. These can be obtained from local hobby shops in your area. New boxes are, however, rather expensive, and I don't think that they're as interesting as what you could find on your own.

A first project shouldn't be too large.

Other Things to Decoupage

Sometimes interesting ideas come about by rummaging through antique and secondhand stores. A sunny spring Saturday found my husband, Jon, and me out looking for unusual objects to decoupage. It really isn't necessary to decoupage a conventional item. Although I generally like things that are useful and have a purpose, this time I was out to try something unusual.

The first place we went to was a local antique shop. I was hoping to find a little chest, something like an oversized treasure chest (my compulsion for boxes!). The first thing that caught my eye was this large old piece used for storing wood. That was really too big to lug home and didn't inspire me, but it was in good condition and could have been done beautifully by someone more ambitious. That shop had many ideas. There were mirrors of all shapes, an old coat rack and an oblong piece of wood with hooks, which must have been a coat rack of some sort. There was a silverware carrier and an old salt holder—you know, the kind of

Bin to store wood is too large a project, but the octagonal box would make an interesting plant holder.

wooden box that held salt and was hung on the wall years ago. I thought that the holder could be done with an ivy design and used to hold matches or a plant or napkins. Almost anything. There were many different-sized boxes, among them a silver chest.

I especially liked the doll-size dresser and thought it could be adorable in a child's room. My favorite find was an octagonal pot. It was painted a horrible green, but it could be repainted and used as a planter. A wooden grain scoop, an old wooden spoon, a hand mirror were some of the other items we saw that were interesting to decoupage. I found an interesting wooden candlestick in the basement, better known as "the dungeon," of an antique shop. It had been stripped down to the bare wood, and I decided that it was too pretty to paint. It seemed just right for a lacy design that might look like filigree and be quite subtle. The decoupage

Doll's chest for little girl's room.

Look what I found in the dungeon of an antique shop! Cutouts were applied right onto the bare wood for a more subtle effect.

process is the same except you do not paint the item first. Just sand and paste the cutouts right on top of the wood.

Next stop in our search for unusual items to decoupage was a real junk yard. We are fortunate to live near the most fantastic house-wrecking company. If you have a good local dump, it can probably serve the same purpose. I searched this place all afternoon for "something that didn't look like anything." It wasn't too difficult as there was everything from kitchen sinks to barber poles to simply nondescript objects. I think this is a great way to find oddities. Jon thought perhaps I could decoupage something that simply didn't have a use or description—just something that could stand by itself, for the sake of itself. Naturally the first thing I spotted was a box. It is an old box to hold spools of thread. I loved it and we bought it.

We also came home with two objects that look like dowels.

You'd be surprised what can inspire you at the local dump.

Maybe I can be creative with these.

I took this one home with me.

They aren't anything that we recognized, so we thought they would be good to experiment with. But I still hadn't found the great object that was to turn into my prize. And then I found it! When looking for something to decoupage bear in mind that it is important, above all else, to like the thing you are going to work on. If you don't care for it, it will be difficult to put your most creative efforts into making it a piece you will be proud of. The "thing" that I found was broken, ugly and in terrible condition. It was the kind of object, if found in your garage, you would pay someone to remove. I had to have it. I wasn't sure what it would be, but I like plants and my first thought was to make it into a planter—even if I wasn't sure which end would be up.

Keep your eyes open. Many things you might discard as having seen better days could have potential.

My "Thing."

You see. It really can be done.
From junk yard to living room.

WHERE TO LOOK FOR CUTOUTS

Once you have decided what you will decoupage you will probably have some subject in mind to place on it. If this isn't so, then the next thing to decide is where to look for cutouts. *Any magazine won't do.* While it would seem logical that your best source of material might come from that which is most readily on hand, it isn't true. Magazines have terrific material, but the paper is often too thin, and when you start to varnish, the print from the other side bleeds through. This is not true of all magazines, however. It is equally important not to use paper that is too thick. When the paper is very thick, many many coats of varnish must be used, which takes a long time. Some magazines with heavier paper, such as *Gourmet* and some travel magazines, may work. Often they have excellent color illustrations of food that make up nicely on a plaque. If you have something that you particularly like, don't despair. I will tell you how to peel backs of too-thick cards and add to too-thin pieces later.

Paper souvenirs, such as menus or tickets, could be arranged on a board or table top or even a dresser top. Old valentines, greeting cards and post cards are really too thick, but a layer of paper can often be peeled off the back, as we'll see shortly.

A woman who watched me demonstrate at a museum show went home and did two plaques as a first project. She called me twice during the time she was working to ask questions. When she was finished, she said she wouldn't part with them for fifty dollars apiece. She made them for her kitchen.

I find the best source for cutouts is your local bookstore. Most bookstores have a section for sale books. This is the part of the store where you should make yourself a permanent fixture. You might also alert the bookstore owner to your needs so that if you are looking for something in particular he or she can call you if it goes on sale. I generally don't recommend buying new books unless there is one that is particularly good and is inexpensive. Book jackets sometimes work, and you might be alert for damaged jackets also available at bookstores. Flowers, birds, butterflies are excellent subjects, as well as figures and animals. Many bookstores in large cities and art supply stores sell separate pages of flower or bird prints, as well as copies of well-known prints that you can adapt to your piece. Museums and some art stores sell reproductions of famous paintings that you might be able to use. If you want to color your own black-and-white pictures, you can do this with water colors or colored pencils that are available in art supply stores. There are also decals sold for this purpose, but I advise against using these. One of the important parts of doing decoupage is to learn to cut out the design yourself. Children's books are another source of cutouts. You could make a charming group of

Books are your best source for cutouts.

plaques from a child's book; the animals and whimsical figures are wonderful subjects. I once decoupaged a photograph of my daughter on a board. I surrounded it with flowers and it is quite cute hanging in the hall.

I usually set a limit for myself pricewise and decide how much I would pay for a single illustration. Then when I find a book and thumb through it I can figure if the price of the book warrants the amount of designs I can use. Sometimes there is a tiny flower or animal in a picture that particularly appeals to me. If the book is one dollar and there is nothing else in the book that I like, I have to decide if that little animal is worth a dollar. If I've been looking and looking for just the right finishing touch for some prize I've been working on, then it is. If the picture just hits my

The cutouts for this baby oval were found in a child's nursery song book.

30

fancy, I usually don't bother. Children's books are good because they are usually filled with possibilities and are inexpensive. The color is good for decoupage. I have two old English flower books that cost $3.98 each, and I've been using them for three years. Keep your eyes open for cutouts at all times.

Jon and I can't resist garage sales, and when we were out photographing for this book we suddenly saw a Tag Sale sign on a telephone pole. We followed the arrows and when we saw this sign on the table in the driveway out came the camera. The old wallpaper sample books were something we hadn't expected to find, but they are excellent for lining

Pieces of discarded wallpaper are excellent for lining boxes.

Using subtle colors.
Handmade boxes by Gramp
decoupaged by Leslie.

Fantasy scene

*A jewelry box looks very elegant
lined with velvet.*

Half round box made by Gramp.

Trinket boxes are delightful first projects because you can see results quickly and they are easy to design.

boxes. There was the usual box of discarded books, but none with pictures that were good enough.

The question I am asked most often is, "Where do you find cutouts?" Everywhere I go I have my antennae up. It gets so that if I see a woman in an especially pretty printed dress I cut it out in my mind and design it on a box.

When we were on the Caribbean cruise, the last port was Bermuda. After the very hot islands of Grenada and Barbados, Bermuda at 60 degrees was cold. Jon and I went shopping, and as with most new towns we visit, we headed for the local bookstore. I wanted to find a book or prints of Bermuda wild flowers. They had many books, but the illustrations were not good enough to use. Remember, always ask in bookstores if they have any prints or loose book pages. We asked for botanical prints and were sent to another bookstore that we otherwise never would have discovered in its tucked away location. I bought some lovely wild flower and English children's books. Each was under two dollars. The shop didn't have any prints that were usable and reasonably priced. Walking to the Princess Hotel for lunch, we came upon a little pink antique shop set back from the road. Pegasus was the highlight of our trip. This tiny little shop was crammed with the most delightful furniture and little wooden objects. Though there were many beautiful prints and flower books, I felt that the prints, at ten dollars, were too expensive to use. You see I don't cut indiscriminately. However, most often when I am working on a box that will be sold I use one-of-a-kind valuable prints. These would have been excellent, but they didn't have exactly what I wanted. While we were at the Pegasus we discovered some little wooden objects that held rouge and lipstick and a perfume bottle. We were told that they are called Treen. We ordered a book about Treen from England as I am always intrigued with unusual wooden objects to decoupage. Sometimes you may go into a shop for one thing and discover something else that you can use for a decoupage project.

"What about the beautiful greeting card I saved, or the wild rose I found in a magazine?" Can you use these for decoupage? I once gave a demonstration of decoupage in a department store, and after I explained the importance of the weight of the paper a woman announced, "You've ruined my whole valentine present." She explained that she had been cutting out and collecting things that appealed to her from magazines. She had an entire collection of memorabilia and had found a large board. She wanted to apply the memorabilia and make a collage effect, using the technique of decoupage. This made me realize that many people might have things already on hand that they would like to use. If you are *starting* to look for something, I still suggest looking for paper that is not too thick or thin. However, I made two suggestions for the lady's valentine cutouts. She could paste the too thin picture to a thin piece of white paper, using white glue. When it was dry she could cut out the design, then apply it to her wood. Or she could paint the back of her magazine picture with white paint, let it dry and then cut out. With this technique you have to be careful to apply a thin coat so that your picture won't curl.

If you wish to use a card that has thick paper, I recommend peeling off a layer of the paper. You can best do this by wetting the back slightly with a damp sponge. Then pull up a corner with your cuticle scissors or finger nail and carefully peel off a little at a time. Take care not to pull off too much or you will tear your picture. Cut out your design after peeling off the layer of paper.

If you find a picture that you like and it is not exactly complete, don't discard it. Work around the problem. For instance: In this design I loved the boy running with the little elf holding onto his foot. The problem was that one foot and one hand were missing because the illustration was at the bottom of the page. I had that boy lying around for months before I could use him. I knew that I would have him running out from behind a tree or bush, but I needed something just right. Often this happens where part of a bird's wing is covered or two animals are standing together and you need only one. Doctor your picture by thinking creatively. Make up a story in your mind to compensate for

A cutout doesn't have to be in perfect condition. The boy has no foot or hand.

the problem. Branches of trees or petals of flowers are great for covering up defects. You can overlap designs, but remember more varnish is needed when the picture is on thicker paper. Of course, you can always eliminate when there is something in a picture that you don't like, and you can also add something else. When I did this lap desk I used an illustration. The flower was very lacy and I hesitated before cutting it up. However, if I used it the way it was, it would seem too heavy and out of balance on one side, and not interesting enough if just placed in the center of the box. I cut it the way I thought it would fit on the top. First, I cut the flower stems where it seemed most logical. This was done where it wouldn't look strange to make two flowers

Finished lap desk. Designs were all one flower.

Move your cutouts around before gluing.

Change and rearrange your design until it looks right to you.

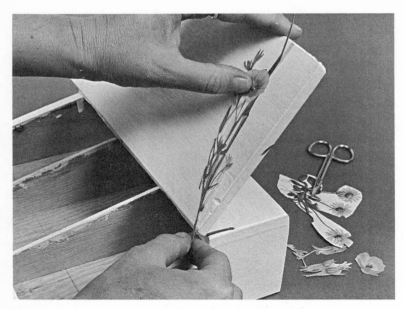

If a cutout doesn't fit exactly, trim it.

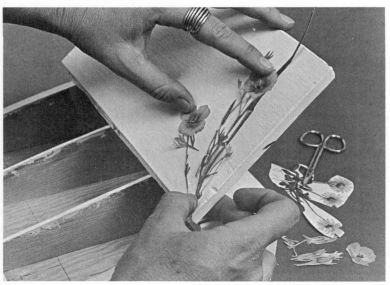

Lay your cutout down in place, stand back and look at it. If the design doesn't look balanced, snip a part off, add it somewhere else.

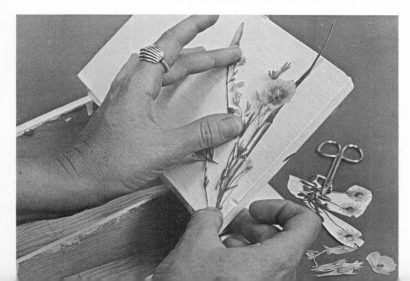

38

out of one. In other words, when you cut up an existing flower—making it look like many or eliminating something—try to do it so that it looks natural. Then when you have a couple of pieces cut off you can start arranging them on the piece. It took me two days of rearranging to achieve the final design. The inside of the top of the desk is made up of leaves from one flower put together with a red blossom of another flower placed on top for color. Often I like the leaves of one plant but the color of the flowering part is not right for my color scheme. So I change it.

For the inside of this lap desk, I added, subtracted, added some more, studied it and changed it altogether. That's the way it goes sometimes. You have to remain flexible.

I changed the entire flower inside and pieced things together.

MATERIALS NEEDED

When you have decided what you are going to make, you should assemble everything you need to make it. Much like making a cake. A very important part of doing a decoupage project before you even get started is deciding where you can work completely undisturbed. That is, where your work can be undisturbed. The actual mechanical process of the work itself takes very little time. Each step—with the exception of cutting—should only take minutes, but the entire project will take a couple of weeks. This is because each process must dry overnight before you continue. The actual time it takes to coat a piece with varnish or paint is very short. However, you should have a place where your work can dry between coats free from disturbance and dust if possible. One of the decoupage artist's biggest hazards is the dust that settles on your work before it has had a chance to dry. This can be taken care of fairly simply when you sand over it the next day. Fingerprints and smudges, however, are not that easy to cover. You do not need more than a shelf that is out of the way if you are working on one small piece. A piece of furniture would be more difficult and you would probably need a workroom.

Everything to make the project easier and therefore more fun.

Item to be decoupaged →

WHITE GLUE
A SMALL BOTTLE
I PREFER ELMER'S

PAINT
WHAT KIND TO BUY
SEE PAINT SECTION

Paint brush

VARNISH

CUTICLE SCISSORS:
(You can't get away with your son's small art scissors that he's cut every thing from construction paper to the dog's hair with!

Cheesecloth or small rag...

2 rags if you are antiquing

mix or buy ↗

Antiquing SOLUTION

SANDPAPER
SEE NEXT SECTION

(I prefer Butcher's clear white bowling alley wax)

CLEAR WHITE PASTE
WAX

STEEL WOOL
000 GRADE

KRYLON
SEE NEXT SECTION

*Most hardware stores will carry
everything you need.*

What and Where to Buy Everything You Need

Almost everything you need is easily obtained in your local hardware or art supply store.

1. *Sandpaper*, very fine black sandpaper—NOT fine, but VERY fine. It is called WetorDry sandpaper and it's made by 3M, but any brand name will do if it is very fine. You will need only one piece of this for a small object such as a plaque or box, but for a piece of furniture you will do well to buy a whole pack for a little over a dollar. You will also need a piece of medium-heavy sandpaper. You would not need a whole pack of this even for a large object.

2. *Small flat paint brush*, natural bristle, not expensive. If you are using oil paint, you might want to use two brushes, especially if you are not superbly talented at cleaning your brush after it has been used for several coats of oil paint.

3. *Krylon*. When I first started doing decoupage, I would spray the entire design, when glued in place, with Krylon. This was to prevent the color from fading, or whatever it says on the can that the stuff does. After a year or so, I kept forgetting the Krylon and soon eliminated it all together. However, while I have never had a box returned to me, I can't say that years and years from now the colors won't all disappear because of my oversight. So, for your first venture you might as well invest the dollar ninety-eight. If you are on a tight budget and don't know if you'll use the Krylon for any other art work, skip it.

4. *Varnish*. Buying varnish is tricky business. Now who would think that buying varnish would be tricky? Well believe me it is. There are all kinds of varnishes and you really have to know what you're doing before embarking on a varnish-buying venture. Here you have another decision to make. What kind of look do you want? Should it be a highly glossy look or a dull sheen? Should it look old or contemporary? I am very prejudiced on the subject of varnish, but before brainwashing you with my prejudices I will do my

best to present all the facts in as unbiased a manner as possible.

There is only one varnish that is *not* right for decoupage. That is spar varnish. This is used for exteriors—almost strictly for boats. Any varnish that says "for interior wood" on the can can be used. There are two kinds of varnish that are especially used for wood. One is high-gloss all-purpose clear varnish, which is fine, does not have to be thinned and can be easily obtained. I prefer the other, which is a satin-sheen varnish. I like my work to have an old look and the satin-sheen gives a matte-like finish. You may try both in this way:

One day I bought the high-gloss varnish by accident and used it before discovering it wasn't what I wanted. It dried more quickly, which is one advantage, but not that quickly. Anyway, I wasn't about to start my project over after going that far, so I put the dull varnish right over the high gloss (after it had thoroughly dried) and it completely covered it as though I had never used the other. My point here is that you can put a coat of one varnish on to see if you like it and the second coat can be the other kind. A small can, pint size, is about a dollar. No matter how much work you intend to do, never buy large cans of varnish because it spoils once the can is open. Remember to close the can tightly. Even then, a film forms on the surface and should be removed each time you varnish. This doesn't happen so much with the all-purpose clear.

5. *Antiquing.* Only if you choose to. Refer to antiquing section before deciding.

Hinges, Catches and All Other Good Things

The hardware store is another favorite place of mine. If you want to add that extra special something to your box, check out the various hinges and catches at your local store. A fancy brass lock or catch can be the touch on your box that makes it look very special. Hardware stores usually carry a variety of brass accessories.

Look for interesting hinges and catches to give a box character.

ALL SET, READY, GO

Often when I'm working on many boxes at once, I find it difficult to remember what stage I'm at. It is just as difficult if you're working on one item if you happen to have either 1) a bad memory, or 2) if you're doing a trillion things, or both, which is my problem. I have, after four years, worked out a solution.

Make a list with every step written down. It could look like this. As you do each step (or repeat) check it off.

The important part is to write down how many coats of varnish have been applied so that you will not lose track and do more work than is necessary.

Chart a work sheet.

Heavy sand					
Paint	1	2	3	4	etc.
Light sand	1	2	3	4	etc.
Last paint					
Cutout designs					
Arrange on article					
Spray Krylon					
Varnish	1	2	3	4	5	etc
Sand	1	2	3	4	5	etc.
And so on . . .					

46

Sanding

Let's begin. I thought we could first work together on a trunk so that you could see each process in progress. Before applying the first coat of paint, sand your piece satin smooth. Be careful with this first step, it will make a big difference in the finished work. Use medium-heavy sandpaper. If you are working on a piece of furniture, remove the old finish enough so that the new paint will go on smoothly (not necessarily down to the bare wood). Rubbing it down first with turpentine will help. Wipe off sandpaper dust with a clean rag or cheesecloth before painting.

The painting and sanding process go hand in hand. After you paint a coat and it dries thoroughly, you will use the very fine sandpaper. After each coat of paint, wet the sandpaper slightly and go over the painted surface for a fine, smooth look before putting on the next coat of paint.

Sand lightly before primer coat.

Painting

When your item is satin smooth you will paint it in the color of your choice. The first coat of paint is your primer coat. I used white on this chest although the final color was to be mustard. Almost any paint will do. You can use whatever paint you have at home. I don't, however, care for a glossy enamel. I have read that enamel is the only paint to use for decoupage and that water-base paint doesn't work at all. I've been using water-soluble paint for years and it works fine. I have used oil paints often, but prefer a latex wall or indoor paint. The oil paint is harder to work with, takes much longer to dry and is messy to clean up. The advantage of oil paint is that there are better colors available for decoupage—many premixed old colors are not available in

Paint in one direction.

water-soluble paints. Also, you don't have to put as many coats of the oil paint on your work. However, I recommend water-base latex paint, especially for a first project. Since the water-soluble or latex paint dries much faster, you can apply two or three coats in one day.

You can get the color you want by either having your paint store man mix it for you or by doing it yourself. The cheapest and easiest way to buy your paint and get the color you want is to buy an inexpensive small can of white latex indoor paint. Then buy the color paint you want in a tube. I buy acrylic paints in tubes at an art store and mix the colors I want. The tubes cost about one dollar. This is how to mix your color: First open the can of white paint and hammer nail holes (about four) around the inside rim of the can where the paint usually collects. This is not necessary of

Three coats of paint were applied over the primer coat.

course, but this is a helpful book, so be patient. Pour off some white paint into an empty jar—not much, just about a quarter of a cup. The excess white paint will drip back into the can where you made the holes and you won't have a sloppy mess. Put the top tightly back on the can. You can always use white paint. Mix in your color from the tube and stir while you do this to get the darkness of color that you want. You can also mix two colors.

Each coat must dry thoroughly before sanding lightly. This is important because if the paint is not dry, it will peel right off and you'll have to sand and start the process all over again.

How many coats of paint you wish to put on is up to you. I recommend at least three or four. You can be the best judge by the way the piece looks to you. If it looks and feels smooth and well coated, then you've done enough. Sometimes the water paint leaves brush strokes, but the wet sanding smooths this out. Use a light hand when painting the final coat. To avoid brush strokes, paint in one direction then, without adding any paint, with the tip of your brush stroke very lightly across the parallel lines of paint.

If you are working on a box, it is not necessary to be terribly concerned about the hinges when painting. I don't recommend slapping paint right over them, but it doesn't matter if a little gets on the hinges. If you are going to antique, the hinges will even look better if you put a lot of antiquing on them. If you don't antique, most of the paint can be sanded off the hinges when you sand the box.

The color you choose is an important decision in designing your piece. I often use white as a background because almost any design looks well on a white background. Even white on white is quite elegant and sophisticated. I used white flowers with green stems on my plant holder. I have another reason for using white more than the other colors. When a white object is decoupaged the result is similar to a piece of ivory. It is amazing how the stark chalky look of the painted white piece slowly takes on an ivory look as more and more coats of varnish and finally the antiquing are applied.

I happen to like the same colors used together, such as the green stems used on a green background. (See Color Plate 1.) The subtleness is quite lovely. Mustard yellow is a good color to work with flowers because many wild flowers are in the orange and yellow colors.

Kind of Brush

I use two different brushes for painting and varnishing, and another for my antiquing. All the brushes are the same size. I use inexpensive brushes because . . .

1. There is nothing like a new brush, and if it's inexpensive, you can throw it away after a short time and get another. Also, a cheap shedproof brush works as well as an expensive one.

2. The brush must be clean, and it is a bother to rush to clean it in turpentine or mineral spirits and then wash it out with soap and water and Lestoil after every one of those twenty coats of varnish.

The size I like best is a flat ½ inch natural camel-hair brush, and when I last bought one it was forty-five cents.

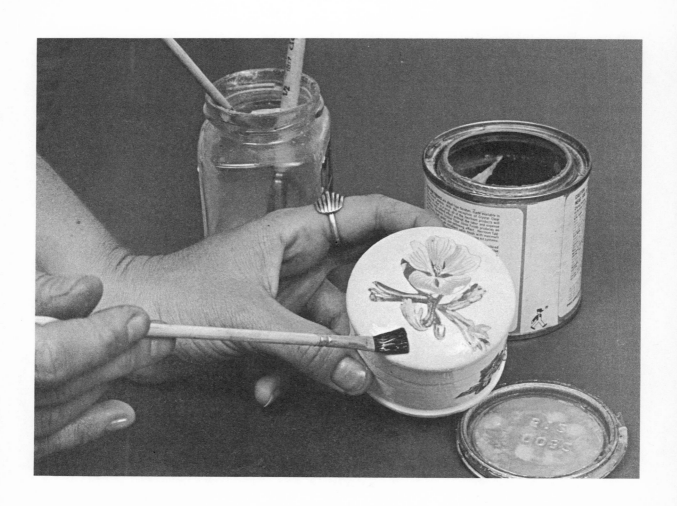

SELECTING A DESIGN TO CUT OUT

The selecting and arranging of a picture is where the fun and creativity of decoupage come about. It is the creating of an appealing scene that gives you the opportunity to have an original piece of art work. You must remember, when selecting what you will decoupage, that you should take your time to select and arrange only that which is exactly right for you, because it takes a long time from beginning to end to complete a piece. It is a lot of work and the end result should reflect this. If you are not selective, you run the risk of losing interest in the project before you are through.

When you select a design remember that it isn't necessary to use the whole picture. For instance, most of the time I find a picture that has one thing in it that I like. Perhaps there is a bird hanging from a flower that I know will be just perfect for the top corner of a box. Or I may combine two flowers or add a leaf where one is needed on a flower that doesn't have one. I take all sorts of liberties in combining my designs to fit my object. So there isn't any real set way to design. It should be what works for you. Look around, see what is appealing to you in your natural surroundings. I use wildflowers primarily. They are so uninhibited that I like to present them this way. That doesn't mean unplanned; just unstiff. I don't think that designs must be realistic. They can be out of proportion in size, and this can be quite charming.

When I designed the box on page 55 I wanted it to be a fantasy, not a realistic design. (See Color Plate 2.) Since it was to have a light feeling, I decided first to use daisies. The daisy is my favorite flower—which, by the way, is a good reason to choose a particular cutout. When you like something it designs well. The daisies grow wild and uninhibited and are light in color and feeling. Also they represent love . . . "she loves me, she loves me not." The stems are not rigid and the leaves are delicate as well as a bit scraggly. I had an old French nursery book that I found in an antique bookstore. The color illustrations of children are delightful and I decided to use them somehow. If you have a book you like, it is a good idea to thumb through it over and over again until something catches your eye. Sometimes the third time through, a corner of an illustration may be just what you needed but overlooked before. There is a psychological problem with books that must be overcome—cutting. When my neighbor first saw me cut into an old, perfectly beautiful and valuable book she said that she couldn't bear to watch me ruin it. But I can't think of a better use for a beautiful illustration than to preserve it in the form of decoupage. That way you can enjoy it every time you look at your finished piece. This is also important. Remember you are creating a piece of artwork, and you should always use designs that you think are beautiful and worthy of the care you will put into it.

In this case, one grouping of children could be cut out "ready made" from a storybook.

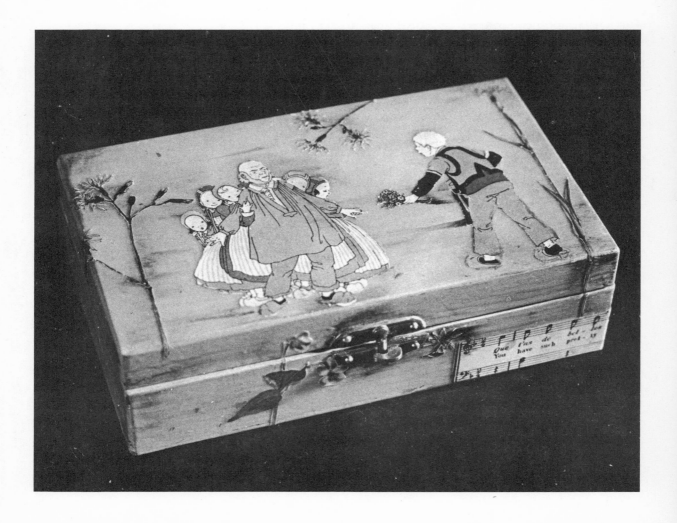

I went through my nursery book dozens of times. I have used it before and find that with each new project I must look at each page of illustrations again and again. Sometimes I have discarded something that I may use later on. I decided to put the children in a field of daisies, and to make it a fantasy or whimsical picture, the daisies would be much larger than the children. So, they would be in what would seem like a jungle of wild flowers. I found a girl sitting and added a young boy, but I wanted her to hold a bouquet in her hand. Of course you can't always find exactly what you want, so you must create the scene that you want. I didn't have a ready-made bunch of daisies for my girl to hold, and chances are if I did, they wouldn't be the exact size that I needed anyway. I cut a small bud from one of the larger flowers. (If there had been no bud, I would have used the petals from another daisy and made my own.) I then cut a stem from another flower. I cut this down to the right size and put it in her hand. The box I chose to put my design on has a curved top. I moved the daisies around until I felt that they followed the lines of the box. I eliminated extra flowers that I felt made the design too crowded and cut off petals and leaves where they got in the way. I moved my children all around; tried them on the front; put them together; put them behind the daisies, peeking through the stems. I re-arranged them until I created the effect that was pleasing to me. In this case I chose the design, in my head more or less, before I chose the object. Sometimes it works the other way around. I used the curve-top box because I didn't want a square, flat-top rigid box, but rather one that was a little unconventional. Also the looseness of the stems flow up and over the curved top so nicely. The color of the box is white. It could have been a buttercup yellow and it would have worked just as well, but I like the subtleness of white on white. Also the girl and boy have blue costumes, and I felt that they would look better on a white background.

It is often necessary to cut out several designs in order to try them before finding one that actually works. It is difficult to look at a page of flowers and guess what they will look like pasted on a box. Very often you will not want to put a flower on your piece the way it appears on the page. Sometimes you will find that part of one flower looks better with a leaf from another. Also, you may want to use only part of the flower or break it up differently. This takes some playing around with and is worth the effort.

Another point, I think you will like the effect best if all the cutouts are of the same thickness.

Cutting

If you are making a design of cutout pieces rather than simply applying a whole picture, you should use small cuticle scissors for cutting. I have tried using an exacto knife and a razor blade and have found that neither do the job as effectively as a cuticle scissors. I don't think that there is a "right" way to cut. What feels best is right for you. You may find that to start in the center and work out is helpful because it enables you to hold the outer page while cutting the center. If you are doing any intricate cutting, you will have to practice a little to cut accurately. I know that sounds like kinder-

Use a sharp cuticle scissors for cutting your paper.

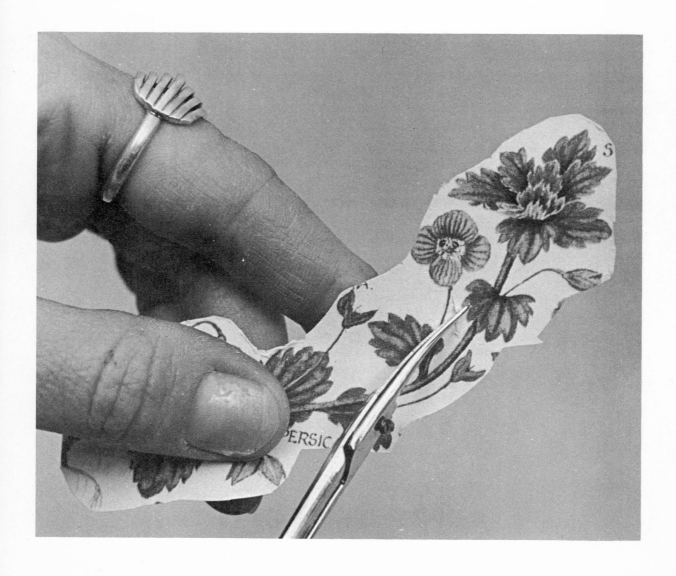

garten craft, but try it. For a first project I would recommend staying away from anything too lacy and small to be cut easily.

When you do cut something very intricate or delicate you can best get into the tiny spaces by using the point of your scissors and poking it in the center. Then work outward from the center of your poked hole until the little space is cut out. It is most successful if your scissors are kept sharp. If you have trouble, you might use a magnifying glass to see the area to be cut. The kind that go around your neck so that your hands are free might work. I've seen them advertised in magazines but have never used one.

Cut the way it "feels" right. You'll find it is easier to control your cutting with the scissors turned away from you.

Placement of Design

Once you have your design cut out lay it down and play with it. Just lay it down on your painted object and look at it. How does each individual cutout look in relation to the size of your piece? Does each piece work with the others to make a pleasing design? Does it flow over your object or is there a spot that is awkward? If so, rearrange, exchange. If a leaf on one of your flowers is out of place, cut it off. Place it elsewhere or discard it. Do not be afraid to experiment. If you have an object that has a rounded top, or curves, don't use stiff designs. Rather, use a lacy vine or a clover with rounded leaves. If you are working on a piece of furniture, don't use a design that is to small for it. Have your design go across the drawers for interest.

Once the design works and you see it, stand back away

A drop of rubber cement will hold your cutouts temporarily in place while you look at them.

from it and look at it again. Squint your eyes and look at it. This enables you to block out distractions. If it looks good, don't hesitate. Go ahead and glue it in place. If there is something wrong with it, but you aren't quite sure what it is, go away from it. Do other things. Come back later and take a fresh look. If it still isn't right, take off the entire design and start over. Sometimes I leave cutouts that I have worked on for ages. I just leave them on my work table for a month. One day I'll walk into my studio, pick up one cutout put it with another, and a design starts to form.

The most important part about designing your object is to learn how to discard. It is hard to discard a cutout that took several hours to cut. You have to force yourself not to use it when you know it just isn't right. However, if you put it aside, you can use it for something else. Remember, decoupage isn't done overnight.

Sometimes you have to cut out many things before you decide on the right "look."

Gluing

Leave your cutout design on your object and take each piece off one at a time to glue. Then put it back in place. I like to use a white glue, and I apply it in many ways. If the piece is not too intricate, such as the top of a flower, I squirt out a drop of glue in the center of the back of the flower. Then I spread the glue evenly with my finger from the center to the outer edges, making sure that there is enough to cover the entire edge. It should be sticky, but not thick so that it won't ooze out of the edges when glued down. When I glue stems or lacy cuttings, I like to put a little on my finger and spread the glue lightly up the back of the stem.

I have found it is best to do my gluing on the kitchen counter top or similar table top. A formica table or a glass surface is good. If you do your gluing on top of a piece of paper, you run the risk of having part of the design stick to the paper when you try to lift it up. After applying glue to the daisies I lifted them up from the end of the stem very gently, peeling the cutout off the table top.

Another way you could do your gluing would be to cut the flowers and glue the parts in place a piece at a time. For instance, the leaves of the daisies could have been snipped at the base near the stem. Then you would first place the stem and daisy and then add the whole leaf where you wanted it to be on the stem.

A third way to glue would be to apply a thin coat of glue with your finger over the area on your box to be used. Then you would lay the design right down over the glue, and with a slightly damp sponge you would pat down the design and wipe off any excess glue as you pat with the clean sponge. It is important to remove all excess glue as it will leave spots when you varnish. When you lay your glued piece in place it is important to be sure that all tiny edges are securely glued down. Also, pat your design down firmly so that there are no air bubbles. This process is much like applying contact or wallpaper.

This is how I apply a design. First I pat my design down firmly with the palm of my hand. I then take my paint brush and lay it across the center of my design. I use it like a rolling pin and roll it carefully to each outer edge. This pushes out air bubbles and any excess glue. I happen to own

Using cutouts from thick enough paper not only allows proper gluing but gives the raised effect visible here.

a wallpaper roller and it can be used for larger pieces, but you can use a rolling pin or any other substitute. (For heaven's sake, don't run out and buy a wallpaper roller, unless you're thinking of repapering a room or two.) Then once again I pat the extra glue off with the sponge. If I am going over a curve or around a corner with a design, I am especially careful not to leave any area raised. Press in and around with your fingernail. If the paper must crinkle to go over a curved part or around a corner, that's all right as long as the creases are absolutely glued down in place. This can be a very interesting detail. After you have varnished over any folds, you can see them, but you can't feel them. It should be smooth.

On my first box I didn't have every edge glued down securely and thought that the varnish would hold down everything that I had missed. I was wrong. Varnish does not stick; it makes it more difficult to glue the missed edge down. So . . . beware! If you have it all glued in place and find an air bubble, you *can* make a slit with a razor blade and squirt some glue under the design, but this is tricky and messy.

When I had all my lacy flowers cut out for my plant holder, I was afraid that they would break or get stuck to my finger or the table when I glued them. This is what I did. I put a little glue on the bottom of each stem and spread it just about an inch up the stem with a paint brush. Then I placed each piece in place on my object and patted it down where it was glued. With the paint brush I spread the glue up the stem a little at a time, patting it in place and dabbing it with a sponge as I went along. I used a small puddle of glue on a piece of paper to dip my paint brush into. (The brush can be washed out with hot water.) This method can be used to apply glue to anything when you don't want to use your fingers. However, it doesn't let you have as much control.

You might find the glue spreads easier if you try adding a drop of water to thin it. I don't usually do this, but it can be done. When lining a box, I never thin the glue because it holds better if the glue is thick.

It is now that you can spray the entire piece with clear Krylon if you wish. Let it dry for a few minutes before going on to varnishing.

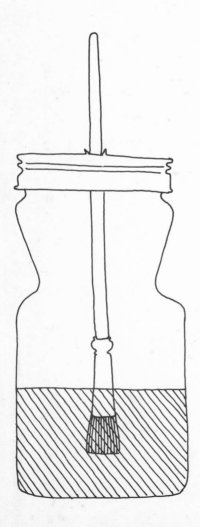

Now you are ready to varnish. As we have seen, there are two kinds of finishes, one very different from the other. There is the superclear, high-gloss finish, which is very contemporary and quite popular. It gives you a very shiny, glossy finish. The other is a satin-sheen, matte finish, which is mellower and has an older, antique quality. Whichever you use is just a matter of personal preference. The brush now is the same kind as you used for painting. If you have cleaned the paint brush thoroughly, you can use it again for varnishing.

Here is a helpful hint for keeping your brush ready and clean for the next varnishing while your piece is drying. This is where that empty olive jar comes in. Take the top off and with a can opener, or some other ingenious implement (a screw driver), make a hole in the top just large enough to push the brush handle through, so that when you put the top back on the brush is hanging in the jar, but not touching bottom. Fill the jar with turpentine or mineral spirits—just enough to cover the bristles. After every coat of varnish you can "hang" your brush in the turpentine. This prevents the bristles from curling over as they would if just left lying in the jar.

After awhile the turpentine becomes gunky and forms a white film. When this happens replace the turpentine and take out the brush and clean it with soap and hot water—or better yet, Lestoil.

I have heard that the only way to varnish correctly is to "float" the varnish on thickly. I have tried this, and there's a lot to be said against that theory. There are, admittedly, a lot of problems that arise when varnishing, but it really isn't difficult. I guess varnishing is just one of those things that is best learned by experience; when you are through with your first piece, you will be well on your way to becoming an expert varnisher. One of the problems is air bubbles. Little bumps, caused by air in the varnish, often appear on your work. This can be alleviated by brushing the varnish on with a heavier hand than you would use for painting. (Believe it or not, you can practically scrub on your varnish.) Simply brush it on in even strokes in one direction, then lightly brush in the other direction with just the tip of the brush. Then put it aside and leave it alone.

That's it. Leave your piece to dry overnight. This is an absolute must. If the weather is damp, it takes longer to dry, and you may have to leave it for two days. It is best to varnish in a warm, dry room. I spend my summers on Nantucket Island, where I sell my work as well as show it in the local galleries. Working one summer against a deadline for the "once every other year craft show" I had the processes timed perfectly. Then we had what I should have been prepared for . . . a week of rain. Never, never apply a coat of varnish over a coat that is tacky. If you put a layer on top of a layer that isn't bone dry, you will have a soft build-up that will peel right off. This was another one of my great goofs that happens only once. When you float varnish on too thickly this is likely to happen. It can be deceiving because although the varnish may appear to be completely dry, it may not be clear down. Also, you run the risk of having the varnish drip down the sides causing drip marks that are not so easily sanded smooth.

When your work is sufficiently dry (if you get stuck, a blower-type hair drier is great) you will sand the whole thing very lightly with black superfine sandpaper. If you have used a fairly thick paper, you should put two coats of varnish on before sanding. Wet the sandpaper slightly and sand. Keep applying coats of varnish in this way until you have achieved enough build-up to cover your design so that it cannot be pulled off. You can repeat the varnish/sanding process approximately ten or more times. I often put twenty coats of varnish on my work. It is really a matter of taste. On a small trinket box, I apply only six or seven coats. When you feel that the design is sufficiently covered so that it feels smooth to the touch, then it is enough. I like the "sculptured effect" of a design slightly raised rather than submerged completely under the varnish, but this is up to you. This is the only part that I can honestly say there is not a short cut for. I know twenty coats sounds like a lot, and it is. There is one way to speed the drying and that is direct sunlight. Recently the sun has been pouring in the studio window, and I discovered that the boxes left on the work table in the sunlight were "set dry" in minutes. This doesn't mean you can varnish right over it, but if you varnish early in the morning you could put another coat on that same night.

The sanding should be done between each coat of varnish, but NOT after the last coat if you are planning to antique.

Address oval on the house
of Mr. and Mrs. Harper Clifford on Nantucket Island.

Cranberry box in a field of rose hips on Nantucket.

Different designs on the same box.

When doing decoupage for the first time you might find it difficult
to get all the materials together and also look for cutouts.
It is important to use the best materials available, and I thought these
old prints were suitable and of help getting you started. I used
the daisy because it is so delicate and you might like a challenge;
if it seems a bit difficult, try the others first. The small ones
are hand-colored copper etchings; the larger, Evening Primrose
is an 1860 stone lithograph.

That step comes next. When you sand, wet the sandpaper slightly before sanding. Then sand very lightly, just enough to take away dust, bumps and slight imperfections.

So, to go over briefly what I've told you about varnishing: It is much better to have more thin coats of varnish build-up than a few very thick coats. Each coat should be bone dry before applying the next coat, and it is a good idea to apply two or even three coats of varnish over your design before sanding. When you sand over the varnish do it with a very light hand so that you will not scratch through to your picture. Wet your sandpaper very lightly—about as wet as a quick lick.

Remember to let your piece dry in a dust-free area. Do not let the top and bottom of your box get stuck together from the drying of the varnish. Prop it open slightly. I use a toothpick to prop open the top. Remember, do not sand your last coat of varnish before antiquing. If you do, it will cause scratch marks and this is where your antiquing solution will settle in rather than where you want to put it.

Prop the box open with a toothpick while varnish is drying.

GET READY TO FINISH

Several weeks have gone by since you began reading this book if you are going along at the rate of progress that I've outlined. If you're wondering if you'll ever finish, perhaps it will warm your heart to know that I'm working on four dozen boxes at once. It isn't easy to remember what step I'm on with each one, and it isn't any easier when you're only working on one item. So don't forget to check on your chart. Otherwise you may forget whether or not you have varnished the last coat on top of the last sanding, and you will end up wasting an extra day because it is better to varnish an extra time than to sand before antiquing.

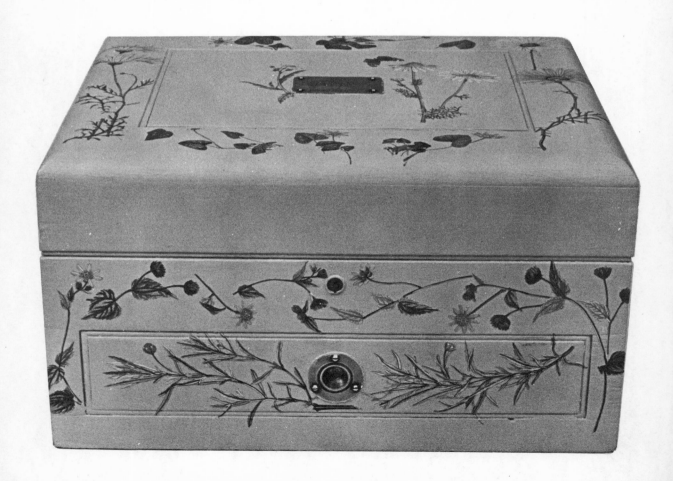

Antiquing . . . Should you? Shouldn't you? Why? Why Not? If you must, how to

Decoupage takes on a completely new flavor when it is antiqued. Antiquing takes a bit of practice. There are various premixed antiquing solutions on the market, or you can make your own by mixing turpentine and linseed oil with equal parts of raw or burnt umber. When you have applied the last coat of varnish remember not to sand. I know I keep repeating this, but it is so important and I don't want you to ruin your piece now that you've gone so far with it. Cheesecloth is an excellent rag for rubbing the antiquing onto your piece. However, any soft clean rag will do. To antique, you should use a clean brush similar to the varnishing brush.

Apply antiquing over the entire design.

Paint the antiquing all over the piece you are working on. Literally cover the design with antiquing. Then with your clean rag wipe off most of the antiquing in this way. First take off most of the "dirt." (The antiquing represents "dirt.") Then try to imagine where the object would be touched the most had it been handled several times. These areas and places where the design is raised are where the most amount of dirt would have accumulated, which is what the antiquing represents. For instance, if you are working on a plaque, the exposed corners or outer edges would be the dirtiest. Therefore, the most antiquing is to be left on the corners. If you are working on a box, it would be on the corners, inside in the corners and, perhaps, in the middle where it would have been handled when opened. I feel that antiquing is a craft by itself and must be done carefully. When working on a box, I use a simple rule before antiquing. I pick it up over and over again to see exactly where to put the antiquing that would seem most natural.

The antiquing should dry thoroughly, again overnight—otherwise you could ruin it by smudging it when you go on to the next step. Another important thing is to be careful not to leave fingerprints on your work when antiquing because when dry they become prominent and permanent. After your piece has dried, put another coat of varnish over the antiquing. This, too, must dry thoroughly.

Antique the hinges to make them look old.

Detail of antiquing on top of chest.

Detail of antiquing in corners and cracks of lap desk.

Your Finished Creation Emerges

Right about now an amazing thing is going to happen. I have made hundreds of boxes, yet I am always surprised at this point. Between this step and the next your work is going to take on an amazing transformation from being incomplete to being absolutely, perfectly, beautifully finished. To get the best results, wet a piece of superfine black sandpaper slightly and sand every part of your work lightly. Then with a piece of 000- or, if you can find it, 0000-grade steel wool go over the piece the same way until you have a satin-smooth finish. Remember to do this very lightly. Don't apply much pressure or you will rub off the antiquing. Wipe off all dust and pieces of steel wool and with a soft rag apply a thin coat of clear white paste wax. I like Butcher's or Johnson's white bowling alley wax. Dry according to the directions on the can and buff until a soft mellow sheen appears.

Half of this chest is antiqued, the other isn't. After the wax has been applied you will have a finished piece of art work, designed and crafted by you.

Lining a Box

When working on a box, I suggest that you think about lining it rather than decoupaging the inside. I have done both, and I think the lined box looks better, unless it is a tiny box such as the little trinket box. I line my boxes with wallpaper. You can probably acquire enough paper to line a box from an old wallpaper sample book that the local paint store is about to discard. Another solution is greeting or wrapping paper. The problem to watch for here is not to get paper that is too thin. It is difficult to line a box with very thin paper because it tears and wrinkles when you apply the glue.

I like to create a surprise with my linings. When choosing a paper for my lining I try to find something that is a contrast in color to my design. Often I pick out the color that is used the least in the overall design and line the box with that color. I usually design with this in mind. For instance, I often use orange and yellow. I may have the box covered with yellow and white flowers with a butterfly fluttering near the flower. There might be a vibrant orange in the wings. I would then pick up the orange color for the lining. Imagine a subtle box with yellow and white on a white background. When you open the box the vibrant orange color leaps out. It creates an exciting touch. (See Color Plates 3 and 4 for similar use of contrasts.)

If I have worked on a small box, I try to use a small overall-patterned wallpaper or greeting paper for the lining. Large bold flowers fight for importance and are distracting. They don't seem to contrast in a complementary way, especially if there are flowers in your design.

You may want to line your box with fabric. I use velvet for a jewelry box. This takes a little more care as each piece must be cut larger than the space it is to fit. The edges will unravel if they are not folded in and glued down first.

Once you have chosen your lining you must assemble all the materials you'll need to do the job. It is really very simple. You will need your glue, scissors and a ruler if you are lining your box with paper.

When you have all your equipment measure all areas to be lined. Since my boxes are handmade, each side is usually a different size and not a perfect measurement. You will not find this so with manufactured boxes. Unfortunately, they lack this charm. Using a ruler and pen I draw each piece to the right dimensions on the paper to be used. Then I cut them out, and using Elmer's Glue, I paste them in place. I do like to cut the sides slightly larger than they measure so that they will overlap a little. The excess can be trimmed later with a razor blade or your cuticle scissors. I put the sides in first and then the large pieces for the inside top and bottom. They should be cut as exact as possible. Lining a box isn't easy at first, so take it slowly and do it when you won't be disturbed. I used to put the same paper as the lining on the bottom of the box, but have since found it is more practical to cover the bottom

These are the materials you will need to line a box.

with felt. This will protect the table the box might be placed on. If you are working on a plaque, you might consider backing it with felt to protect the wall as well as to give your piece a finished look.

You would cut the felt the same way as the wallpaper lining. Put the box right on top of the piece of felt and draw around the box with a pen. Cut the square out and apply glue directly to the bottom of the box. Make sure there is enough on all edges. Place the felt piece on top of the glue and smooth it down with your hand. If there are any edges that are a little too big you can trim them with a razor blade or cuticle scissors.

Look at your box and decide what paper will go with it for the lining.

Once again you open up that trusty varnish can and apply right over the lining. The lining needs only one coat of varnish, and then you can antique it if you decide you want to. The inside need not be antiqued, but I think it is more consistent with the outside. Put a coat of varnish over the antiquing, let it dry, sand and rub with fine steel wool. Apply wax inside the same way you did to the outside.

I suggest that if you are working on a box, you line the box before you start varnishing the outside. Then you can varnish the inside and out at the same time, propping it open slightly so that it dries inside and out. This saves time. Do not prop it open too much or the top will have drip

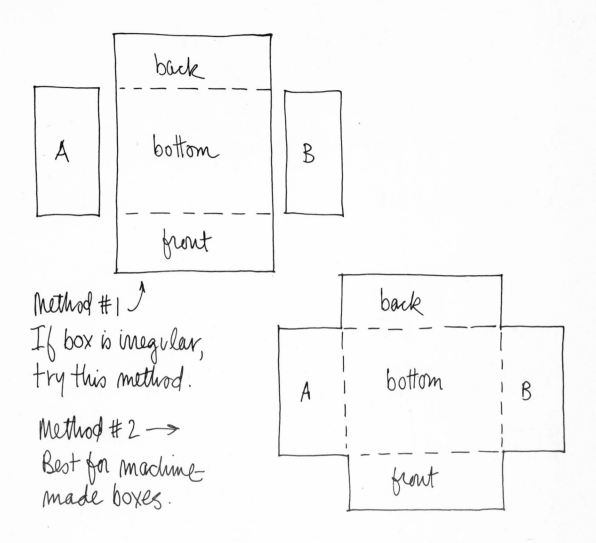

back

A   bottom   B

front

Method #1 ↗
If box is irregular,
try this method.

Method #2 →
Best for machine-
made boxes.

back

A   bottom   B

front

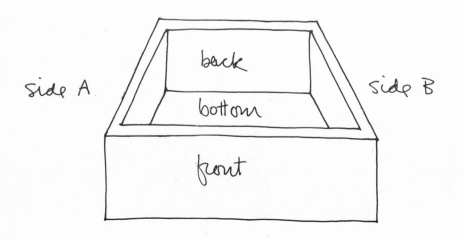

side A   back   side B

bottom

front

marks. I have found that it's a good idea to put the felt on the bottom after the whole box is completed, waxed and all. This will keep the fuzz from the felt from sticking to the box.

If you decide to line your box with fabric, this is how to do it. You can cut each piece out larger than the area to be lined. Then cut pieces of cardboard the exact size for each side of your box. You will then apply glue to one side of each piece of cardboard, one at a time, and glue it to the wrong side of each piece of fabric. Fold edges of fabric over the card-

Lining before antiquing.

board and glue to cardboard to keep edges from ravelling. Apply glue to the back side of each piece and press it in place in the box. You must take special care that each piece fits exactly. Try it in place before gluing. Keep your fingers clean or you will get glue on the outside of the fabric, and it is difficult to remove. You can pat out the glue with a damp sponge, but velvet will remain stiff in that spot. You could also use felt. This is easier because since felt doesn't ravel you can cut each piece to fit exactly. You could even use contact paper for a lining.

Antiqued lining.

MORE ON DESIGN

As you must know by now, I feel that the technique of decoupage can be applied toward creating all kinds of decorating accessories. You can turn a relic into a thing of beauty, you can create all sorts of gifts, and best of all you can be creative without being an artist. You can take a plain, uninteresting, raw piece of unpainted furniture and turn it into a priceless decorated piece. The technique, once mastered, can be applied in almost any way.

Once you have tried various designs and find that they work for you, you will begin to develop a style that reflects your individuality. There will be something recognizable about your work that sets it apart and gives it character. This comes about when you are creating your own designs rather than copying that which has been done before.

When my work first appeared in *McCall's* magazine they had asked me to experiment with a different style. They thought perhaps it would be fun to see how typographic design would work on a file box for a man's desk. I chose a chocolate-brown color, although I thought that a creamy white would work well also. I found bold letters on the front and back cover of a catalogue. Since the letters were off-white, I used a brown background. When I finished I thought it looked well, but it wasn't my style so I wasn't very pleased with it. It just didn't have my signature. Also, I felt that since decoupage is a traditional craft, it should not look contemporary. I think that decoupage can have a creative new look without losing a traditional feeling. The other box that I did at the same time was a small red, white and blue stamp box. This box was painted carefully with three stripes, and I used red, white and blue American stamps to design it. (They could have been French stamps as well.) Then I lined it with American eagle wallpaper. Again, I wasn't thrilled with the results for the same reason.

That is not to say that it should not be done. It is really a matter of taste. This just isn't my style. It may be yours. The magazine did not use them, but used six of my own nature-oriented boxes.

I like decoupage to be antiqued. This gives the piece a particular character, and it looks silly to antique a contemporary design. After all, antiquing represents age. If it is to be a contemporary design, let it be now, right this minute. Don't antique it.

If you have a collection of memorabilia, you might want to work it into a design or collage using the technique of decoupage. Do experiment with new ideas. Try a wedding invitation decoupaged on a plaque, or just do an object for art's sake. It should always be fun.

CHILDREN AND DECOUPAGE

Lately I have received many letters from young people who are interested in decoupage. It occurred to me that decoupage is a marvelous craft for children since the materials and process are familiar to them. After all, children have been painting, pasting and cutting since nursery school.

I do not recommend decoupage for children under seven years old because it is difficult for them to maneuver the scissors. If little children are learning decoupage, or you are teaching a class of children under twelve, I recommend selecting large pictures to be cut. It would be easier if they started with a very simple project.

Rock by Lisa Brunhuber, age 12.

It is important to have the children select a project they like and will be proud of when it is finished. My daughter Lisa decoupaged a rock. First she found a really great rock. What's a really great rock? This one was white, about as big as a fist and pretty smooth on one side. She cut out the little figures from a Joan Walsh Anglund book and pasted them on top of the rock. She didn't paint the rock at all. After she pasted the pictures on with white paste, she put a coat of varnish over the picture. Then she set it aside to dry overnight. In the morning she put another coat on the rock. When she thought the picture felt smooth she sanded the rock very carefully with fine sandpaper. This is a very good way to start doing decoupage because the project is finished before too long. This is important with children. They should see the finished results quickly. A small round piece of felt could be glued onto the bottom of the rock, and it could be used as a paperweight.

I thought it would be fun to show some original work done by children of different ages. I worked with them in regard to finding materials and made a few suggestions for them to get ideas, but their ideas are original, and the work was done by each artist with no more than a little instruction from me. I think the projects are representative of each child's age and personality.

Lisa's plaque.

Lisa is twelve. She made the rock. She is quite creative and wanted to make something for her room. I had collected some odd pieces of wood left over from a panelled room. Lisa decided to use one of the squares of wood for a wall hanging. She had a birthday card that she especially liked. It was a picture of a little girl and there were some flowers as well. I suggested that she cut out the entire square that contained the picture and paste it on the center of the wood, but she decided to be more creative. She cut out the little girl and then each individual flower, using my cuticle scissors. Then she arranged the girl and flowers, making a new scene on the wood. When she had a pleasing arrangement, she glued the picture down on the board with Elmer's Glue. She put about six coats of varnish over the picture, letting each coat dry thoroughly. Lisa could have first painted the board a color for a background, but she decided that she liked the natural wood color best. Of course the whole project would have had a different appearance all together had she chosen to paint it. But the natural wood does look just right with the brown and yellow colors of the girl and flowers. She did not bother with antiquing. I don't feel that a project done by a child should be antiqued. This is a difficult art, and children's things look better if they are not antiqued. Lisa screwed a brass ring into the top and it was ready for hanging. The brass rings for plaques can be purchased for about forty cents in a hardware or art supply and frame shop.

Peter is almost ten. He really didn't know what he wanted to make. He knew only one thing for sure—he didn't want to make anything that anyone else was making. Peter has a good sense of design and has original ideas. He likes to draw abstract designs and has a good feeling for color. I suggested that he make his own design rather than cutting out something from a book or card, etc. Together we came up with the idea of a pendant for his neck. I found a wooden disc that had been the top of a box, and it just happened to have a hole right near the top. This was perfect to put a chain through. (Objects around the house are a good source of ideas for projects. A wooden spoon handle, for instance, could be done.) Armed with Magic Markers and a piece of white paper, Peter used the kitchen table for his studio. First he placed the disc on the paper and drew a circle around it. Then he cut out the circle. He used the entire piece to make a design that would be pasted over the surface of the wooden disc. Then he decided to paint the surface of the other side of the disc. He wanted it to be blue, but I had only a few bottles of water-base paints, and blue wasn't one of them. So, not that I wanted to thwart creativity, he used shocking pink. While the paint dried he made his design with Magic Markers. The paint was fairly thick and only one coat was necessary. Peter pasted the circle of paper with the design on the unpainted side of the disc. Since it was a little larger than the disc, he trimmed it all around with the cuticle scissors. On the pink side he placed another design, which he made to fit just the center of the disc. He explained that when you wear a necklace it usually turns over when you're running, so it really should be finished on both sides.

Pendant by Peter Aron, age 9½.

With Peter I tried an experiment with the varnish. I had a can of spray varnish that I had wanted to try, so we sprayed it on both sides. Then we stuck a pencil in the hole in the disc and placed the other end of the pencil in a jar so that the disc could dry on both sides at once. The can said that the spray dries in thirty minutes, is a satin-sheen finish and will not form bubbles. It took all day to dry, was a high-gloss finish and formed into millions of bubbles. So much for spray varnish. When it was dry Peter sanded both sides and brush varnished again with our good old satin-sheen wood varnish in a can. With this sort of project many coats of varnish are not needed. The paper is thin—regular composition paper. The design covers the entire piece of wood on one side and is quite small on the other. It is entirely up to the child, however. If he would like to apply many coats of varnish, this will produce a hard and smooth finish, but if he loses interest, it is better to finish the project with only two coats. We found a chain from something else and completed the job. I think that you can buy a chain in the desired length in a five and ten, fabric shop or hardware store.

Robby is the youngest to try decoupage. She is eight, going on nine. The first project she did was a very simple one that is quite good for a young child. She took one of the pieces of wood, like the one Lisa used, and painted it white. Then she cut out an entire picture from a book I had found in Bermuda. She chose the picture that most appealed to her, centered it and glued it down. With a whole picture such as this it is a good idea to roll on the picture—with a pencil for instance. After the picture is pasted down roll a pencil on it from top to bottom to get out the air bubbles and excess glue. Robby varnished her picture several times. Her project took about a week. She kept adding coats of varnish. She would put a coat on every day when she came home from school. Since she had started her project before anyone else she wanted to do another. For this she took an oval board that I had in the studio. She wanted to use this and decided to put her name on it for her bedroom door. She cut letters out of a magazine, which I usually don't recommend. However, she used letters that were red and orange, and I didn't think that the print from the other side would show through. We were lucky. It didn't. This was varnished and a brass ring added for the final touch.

"Robin" door sign by Robby Brunhuber, age 8.

Michael is fourteen and a drummer, but this time decided not to do anything about incorporating his musical talents with decoupage. At Christmas time Mike lettered the word "Beautiful" as an art class project. It took a little searching to find something to inspire him. A couple of years ago I found a terrific hunk of wood on the beach in Nantucket. I like pieces of wood, as you may have gathered, and I always manage to have odd pieces around. (I once made a collage of different shapes of wood that I found in a garbage can in Nantucket.) This particular hunk of wood had been on the beach for a long time and was quite weather beaten and just right for Mike's inspiration. He wanted to cut out the "B" from "Beautiful" and use it on the wood. This would be hung with picture wire screwed into the back. It is rather rugged and natural looking.

Steve is twelve and seven eighths. He was the first one with an idea. His thing is music. His entire world revolves around dreams of amplifiers. He plays the guitar. Steve found a beautiful big rock that I thought could be used as a door stop. I think he just wants it to be a big rock. He made letters on paper and cut them out. When he pasted them on the rock it read, "Make Music Not War." I wanted him to put some notes of music on the rock, or at least to add something, but he liked it just the way it was. So here it is. A huge rock by Stephen Aron.

Rock by Stephen Aron, age 12.

The letter "B" designed and
decoupaged on wood by Mike
Aron, 14.

Amy, who is ten and a half made a box that we can't photograph because she sold it to a store. (She's the business-minded one.) It was decorated with charming animals and lined with greeting paper. Last summer in Nantucket Amy and Lisa bought wooden buttons in the thrift shop and decoupaged them to use on a sweater. Amy started a collection of glass animals and Gramp made a box to display them. She is working on a design to trim the outside.

Perhaps the kids' projects will suggest that any work you do with children should be kept simple. You can use materials that the children might find around the house or on the beach. Most of all, they should work on something that is right for them, and each child likes a different thing. It is also a good idea to give as little direction as possible or it isn't as much fun for the kids.

Amy Brunhuber, age 10, painting box to display glass animals.

COMMON FALLACIES

According to various books on decoupage, it would seem that this is a terribly involved and complicated craft. I have also found that for every simple step I have taken, there is a much more complicated way to do it.

The Glue Fallacy

Take the simple act of gluing paper to wood. One would think that by using Elmer's Glue and pasting a piece of paper to the wood, it would be stuck there fairly securely in a matter of minutes. It says so on the jar. Yet most books on decoupage and refinishing furniture say that your design should dry overnight. However, I apply my varnish almost as fast as I can open the varnish can and clean off my brush. I have always done this with no difficulty at all, provided the design is applied firmly, patted down and any excess glue wiped off.

The Unvarnished Truth about Varnish

Varnishing is a subject about which whole books could be written. Contrary to popular opinion, varnishing isn't very difficult. I have been using an old can of varnish all week, dipping my brush through a hole in the hard surface that has formed on the top because I haven't had the time to go out to buy another can. My brush is immaculate though! I don't recommend using old varnish, but in an emergency it can be done. It's true that there is nothing that delights me more than opening a fresh new can of varnish. However, it really does spoil so buy it only in small pint sizes even if you're doing a lot of work. To avoid the hard surface that forms from exposure to the air, I sometimes pour the varnish into a glass jar and turn it upside down when not in use. That way the film forms on the bottom.

Paint

There are many paints on the market that state that they are specifically for decoupage. It is not necessary to use these, and they are usually expensive. Remember, decoupage has been around a lot longer than we have had cans marked "for decoupage." Enamel is not the only paint you can use for decoupage—in fact, I think it is the worst. Brush strokes do not only appear in water-soluble paint, but in oil as well. However, they can be sanded smooth.

Finish

This is also true about finishes. There is no such thing as only one kind of decoupage finish that comes in a can marked "decoupage finish." Varnish is the best wood finish you can apply. Any varnish that says "interior wood varnish" on the can can be used. It is a hard finish, will not get water stained (unlike shellac) and will last forever. It only needs to be protected by a clear wax about every six months.

Hinges

I have read directions for removing hinges from a box that you intend to paint. This is not in any way necessary or advisable. I suggest that you be careful not to slop paint haphazardly over the hinges. However, if a little paint gets on them it doesn't matter. If you are antiquing, you can cover up the paint with the antique mix. This will, in fact add to the character.

WHERE DO WE GO FROM HERE

You keep looking and looking. Looking for things to decoupage. Looking for cutouts. Looking around for design ideas. Most of all, doing. Trying new ways to arrange designs. Experimenting with something you might be tempted to discard.

I know that decoupage takes a bit of time and patience, but I really feel that the results are worth the effort. I also believe that decoupage is a lot of fun. To take a piece of wood or glass or metal and see it slowly go through a metamorphosis is rather exciting and can give you a great deal of creative satisfaction. So . . . enjoy!

WHERE TO FIND THINGS

New Boxes: Hobby shops are springing up all over and they carry new wooden boxes. Also many toy shops and needlecraft shops carry boxes.

A mill will make a good wooden box (pine) any size you want. Be accurate when giving dimensions.

Old Boxes and Other Interesting Objects: Thrift shops
A great aunt's attic or cellar
Tag sales
Goodwill shops
Antique shops

Plaques: Lumberyards
Mill shops
Hobby shops, toy stores (Don't use composition board; it doesn't compare to the real thing.)

Hooks for Plaques: Hardware stores
Art supply stores
Frame shops

Krylon: Art supply stores

Cutouts: Everywhere—bookstores, tag sales, antique shops, greeting card stores, museums.

In New York City: Brandon Memorabilia, Inc., 3 West 30th Street.

Museums for reproductions of famous paintings.

Art and bookstores in large cities often carry cutouts and sell pages from books for decoupage. For instance, you can often buy a whole page of just butterflies or birds without having to rummage through an entire book for what you want. Of course, a page is usually cheaper than buying the whole book, but not always. Keep an eye out for book sales.

Go to antique or craft shows in your area. Sometimes I pick up prints this way.

Wrapping paper sometimes works.

More on Decoupage: If you are ever in Bermuda, look up Pegasus. On Nantucket Island, Massachusetts, Anton's is a marvelously well supplied print shop.

For the history of decoupage and more on technique, *Decoupage*, by Patricia Nimocks, is published by Scribner's.

My favorite book for learning more about wood and finishes is *The Furniture Doctor*, by George Grotz, published by Doubleday. Even though I don't agree with everything Mr. Grotz says, what he says, he says well.

For information on complete decoupage kits write:
The Whole Works! Box 447 Westport, Connecticut 06880